WHY I WROTE THIS BOOK

Life Is Full of Exciting "Firsts."

This is the first volume of *The Tweeters' Handbook*. These books will be filled with many of the "Tweets" from my "Twitter" account. As I have been involved with "Tweeting" I have discovered a new outlet for sharing hundreds of my Wisdom Keys. I never know when The Holy Spirit will bring these inspirational thoughts to my *Mind*. So during my very busy schedule, I simply "Tweet" them to my many friends around the world.

"Twitter" is a powerful social networking service that you can use to send and receive messages known as "Tweets" to your friends or anyone interested in knowing what you are doing or have to say.

"Tweeting" has been a phenomenal means for me to express my message to hundreds and even thousands who want to keep up with me. I may be awaiting an international flight in Rio de Janeiro, Brazil, one minute, enjoying breakfast with one of my dear friends about ready to go on the air for a telethon. I may even be in another country, the next time back home or sitting at my desk at midnight.

I can be a thousand places and be "Tweeting." Twisdom Keys are constantly coming to my Mind and I share them right from my heart unrehearsed...with my friends and partners. *"Twitter" Is Proof...God Can Bring Anyone Into*

Your Life In 24 Hours.
    I know you are going to be inspired and mentored...as you allow these Twisdom Keys to *enter* your *Mind* and life.
    That is why I wrote this book.

Mike Murdock

Unless otherwise indicated, all Scripture quotations are taken from the King James Version of the Bible.
The Tweeters' Handbook, Volume 1 · ISBN 1-56394-437-5/B-297
Copyright © 2010 by **MIKE MURDOCK**
Publisher/Editor: Deborah Murdock Johnson
Published by The Wisdom Center · 4051 Denton Hwy. · Ft. Worth, Texas 76117
1-817-759-BOOK · 1-817-759-2665 · 1-817-759-0300
You Will Love Our Website..! WisdomOnline.com

TW1 My #Thoughts: Honor...Is The #Seed That Flourishes In *Every* Environment.© So I Want The Spirit To Help Me *Master* The "Law of Honor." Solves 90% of Problems.
#drMM

TW2 God's WILL...Is Not A Divine #DECISION. He Wants You Saved; But It's Not His Decision. *It's Yours.* #God Never Makes YOUR Decisions.©
#drMM

TW3 How To Discern Character In Others:
1) Find The Voice They *#Trust*...
2) The Hero They Most *Admire*...
3) Whose Counsel They *#Honor.*©
#drMM

TW4 CONVERSATIONS:
The Only Thing God Does...*Is #Talk.*
He Rules His World Thru...Conversations.
Conversations...Decide Your Feelings/Goals/#Seasons.©
#drMM

TW5 Master Secret: When You #Teach

Your Child To Honor You—You *Guarantee* The #Favor of God On Them For Their *Entire* Lifetime.© (Ex20/Ep5) EXCEL Here. #drMM

TW6 Disinterest....Is An #Instruction. (Jesus Told Disciples To *Withdraw* From Homes Where They Were Not Valued.) #Sow Your Presence *Carefully.*© #drMM

TW7 #PRESENCE....Is A #Seed. Assess *Reactions* of "Soil" (#Environment) You Enter. Are You Ignored? Discerned? Embraced?
#Reactions Reveal Discerning.© #drMM

TW8 Those Who Do Not Improve In My Presence...*Disqualify* Themselves For It.© #drMM

TW9 Presence *Ignites*...Energy, #Honor, Guilt Or #Fear And A Host of Invisible Emotions. Sow Your Presence Carefully. *Analyze* Your #Harvest.© #drMM

TW10 #KINGLY_ANOINTING: Staying #Poised In Environments of #Disrespect. Never Leave Your Chariot To Punish The Peasant Who Throws The Tomato.©
#drMM

TW11 SEASONS Are NOT Decided By God/Pain/Time, But By...Decisions... Conversations...#Mentorship...Loss...Goals... Passion...#Obedience...#Honor.©
#drMM

TW12 #MONEY...Is Not A Miracle, Nor A Mystery. Money Is Simply A #Reward For Solving A #Problem For Someone.©
#WKMM (Wisdom Keys of Mike Murdock)
#drMM

TW13 QUESTIONS:
Jesus Said, A.S.K. I Never Seek Answers. Questions "Introduce" You To Answers... Their "Employees." Labor...To Ask *Great* Questions.© #drMM

TW14 If You...Had Only One Year Left To Live...What Would You Do *Differently?*

Who...Would You Teach? Love? #Comfort?
#Reach For? Forgive? Exits Matter.©
#drMM

TW15 What Is The True Cost of The
#Future You #Dream About? What Must
You Change To *Qualify* For Your Future?
Preparation Is Proof of #Passion.©
#drMM

TW16 Money Is Not The "Only" Reward
For Solving A #Problem:
1) #Favor
2) Worthiness
3) Commendation
4) #Promotion
5) #Recognition
6) #Honor.©
#drMM

TW17 5 Proofs of Love:
1) Willingness To *Listen*
2) Relentless *Reaching*
3) *Passion* To #Pleasure
4) *Desire* To Protect
5) *Refusal* To Betray.©
#drMM

www.twitter.com/DrMikeMurdock

TW18 EVERY MAN...Has Both A #King And A #Fool Within Him; The *One* You Talk To Is The One That Responds.©
#drMM

TW19 Someone You Are #Trusting...May Be Trusting Someone You Would Not.©
#drMM

TW20 The 3 Ways To Know Someone:
1) *Hire* Them...
2) #*Marry* Them...
3) Tell Them *"No."*©
#drMM

TW21 Your #Mind Is The Garden of Your Life. YOU Are The Gardener Who *Plants* Flowers...*Pulls* Weeds...*Kills* Snakes/It *Grows* Your Life_Fruit.©
#drMM

TW22 THE_#HOLY_SPIRIT...Is The Only Person Capable of Being *Contented* With You. He Is *Comfortable* With Your History And Requires No Explanations.©
#drMM

TW23 DON'T HURRY....Away From The Present #Moment; It Took You A Lifetime To Get Here.© From My Book, *The Unhurried Life*. #drMM

TW24 LINGER LONGER...In The Present #Moment; It's The #Future You Have Been Telling Everyone About For Years. *S-a-v-o-r It.*©
#drMM

TW25 If You Get To Where You Are Going...*Where Will You Be..??*©
#drMM

TW26 WHAT DOES IT TAKE...*To Stop You..??*©
#drMM

TW27 SEEDS: Words Are Seeds For *Feelings*. #Listening Is Seed For *Learning*. #Knowledge Is Seed For *Change*. #Conversation Is Seed For *Understanding*.©
#drMM

TW28 QUESTION FOR #SINGLES:

Who Would You #Marry If You Were *Blind?* Do You *Trust* Their History of #Decision_Making? What Are Your *Unspoken* #Fears?©
#drMM

TW29 DECISIONS...Created Your *Present.* NEW Decisions...Will Create Your #*Future.*©
#drMM

TW30 INVEST...Where You See #Gratitude.©
#drMM

TW31 TIME...Does Not Create Change. DECISIONS...Create #Change.©
#drMM

TW32 Unwillingness...To #REACH... Disqualifies You...To #RECEIVE.©
#drMM

TW33 Never Complain About What You Permit.© #drMM
(Quote From Bk...*1,001 Wisdom Keys of Mike Murdock...*WisdomOnline.com)

TW34 Men Do Not #Marry The Woman Who Turns Them ON...
...They Marry The Woman Who Doesn't Turn Them OFF.©
#drMM

TW35 EVERY #MOMENT...Has A Divine Distinction. #JOY...Is The *Immediate* #Reward For Discerning It.©
#drMM

TW36 Plan Your Pleasures...
...Because #Pain *Will* Schedule Itself.©
#drMM

TW37 AN INSTRUCTION...Is The *First* Proof of #Trust.©
#drMM

TW38 You Will Never Attract...What You *Need.* You Will Never Attract...What You *#Love.* You Will ONLY Attract...What You #HONOR.©
#drMM

TW39 The Quality of Your Search...Reveals The *Depth* of Your #Passion.© #drMM

TW40 FATHERS: If Your #Presence Makes A Difference...
Your *Absence* Makes A Difference.©
#drMM

TW41 SEED_TALK:
#Confession Is Seed For *#Mercy*.
#Sleep Is Seed For *#Hope*.
#Endurance Is Seed For *Opportunity*.
#Honor Is Seed For *Access*.©
#drMM

TW42 WOMAN Is To Man...What #God Could *Not* Be.©
#drMM

TW43 EVERY #PROBLEM...Is *Simply* A #WISDOM Problem.©
#drMM

TW44 #Mothers...Decide What Children REMEMBER.
#Fathers...Decide What Children #BELIEVE.©
#drMM

TW45 The Most *Important* Verse In The #Bible Is...Numbers 23:19.
#drMM

TW46 Worship...Corrects Your *Focus*.
#Focus...Decides Your *Feelings*.
#Feelings...Affect Your *Decisions*.©
#drMM

TW47 You Are Not Designed...To #CHANGE Someone.
You Are Not Designed...To UNDERSTAND Someone.
You Are Only Designed...To #LOVE Someone.©
#drMM

TW48 When You Open Your #Mouth, I Know Your #IQ.©
#drMM

TW49 #God Often Hides Something You Desperately Need In Someone You Do Not Enjoy.©
#drMM

TW50 #God...DESIGNS Your #Future. You...#DECIDE Your Future.©
#drMM

TW51 Some Speak...To Be Heard. Some Speak...To Be UNDERSTOOD.©
#drMM

TW52 An #EXPERIENCE With #God... ...Is Not A #RELATIONSHIP With God.©
#drMM

TW53 Everything Created...SOLVES A #PROBLEM.
(Eyes See. Ears Hear. Mind Thinks.) YOU Are Proof God Saw A Problem Nobody Else Can Solve But YOU. #DISCERN It.©
#drMM

TW54 "TWITTER" Is Proof...#God Can Bring Anyone Into Your Life In 24 Hours.©
#drMM

TW55 YOUR #WEAKNESS...Creates #Success For Someone.©

ie. Mechanic-Fixes The Car You Can't.
Interpreter-Translates The Language You
Can't Speak.
#drMM

TW56 Every #Warrior... *Needs* A Nest.©
#drMM

TW57 What You Can Tolerate...You Will
Not Change.©
#drMM

TW58 #Distrust Is Often A #Seed For
#Safety.©
#drMM

TW59 Rewards of An #Enemy:
~Expose The *Judases* In Your Life.
~Makes You Attentive To *Accuracy.*
~Confirms #*Loyalty* of True Friends.©
#drMM

TW60 #Chaos...Is When You #Create
Faster Than You Can Organize.© #drMM

TW61 WISDOM...Is The Ability To

Discern Difference
(In #People/Moments/Environments)
...Is Ability To *Anticipate* A Consequence/
Reward.© #drMM

TW62 Anything Permitted...Will Increase.©
(#Abuse/#Disrespect/Delays...)
#drMM

TW63 Become Skilled At #RECEIVING.
It Decides Your #Giving.©
(How Do You Receive/React To #Gifts/
Access/Opportunities/Correction?)
#drMM

TW64 #SILENCE....Is Permission.
#Abuse.
#Government.
#Bullying.
#Injustice.©
#drMM

TW65 CIRCLES of #PEOPLE...Who
1) You Need
2) Need You
3) Motivate You

4) Comfort You
5) #Mentor You
6) #Trust You
7) Critique You
8) Enjoy You
9) Explore You
10) Admire You.©
#drMM

TW66 #SINGLE_TALK:
It Is *Easy* To Find...The *Lovable.*
It Is *Difficult* To Find...The *#Trustworthy.*©
#drMM

TW67 3 Reasons You Need #Jesus
You Need...
1. #Forgiveness
2. #Friend
3. #Future.©
#drMM

TW68 #Forgiving Someone...Does Not
Change THEM;
#Forgiveness #Changes YOU.©
#drMM

TW69 A Manipulator...Is Uncomfortable With #Truth.©
#drMM

TW70 3 SIGNS of MATURITY...
~Can Listen To Ignorant w/o Responding
~Wrong #Friendships End Quicker
~Don't Feel Responsible For #Decisions of
   Others.©
#drMM

TW71 #Forgiveness...Does Not Restore #Trust.©
#drMM

TW72 #Eagle_Talk: THE ASTONISHMENT of #EAGLES...
Is That Chickens Are So *Contented* In Their Barnyard.©
#drMM

TW73 The #Instruction To *#Forgive*...Was Not An Instruction To *#Trust.*©
#drMM

TW74 "TWITTER"...Creates #Humility.

...It Shows You How Quickly You Can Be Replaced.
...It Reveals How Uninteresting Your Own #Life Is.©
#drMM

TW75 Chemistry...Is Not #Love.
#Desire...Is Not Love.©
#drMM

TW76 #God_Facts
God Does Not Respond To #Pain.
God Does Not Respond To #Tears.
God Does Not Respond To Thoughts.
God *Only* Reacts To...#FAITH.©
#drMM

TW77 #GREATNESS Can Be Discerned...By Its *#Reaction* To...Small.©
#drMM

TW78 #WRONG_PEOPLE:
...Can Last Your Lifetime
...Never Leave Your Life Voluntarily
...Create Sad #Seasons
...Thrive On Misplaced #Mercy.©
#drMM

TW79 When #God Wants To #Bless You,
He *Brings* A Person Into Your Life.
When God Wants To #Protect You,
He *Removes* A Person From Your Life.©
#drMM

TW80 YOU WILL BE REMEMBERED...
For Two Things In Life:
1) The #Problems You *Solve*...Or
2) The Problems You *Create*.©
#drMM

TW81 STRIFE IS PROOF...
~Someone Does *Not* Belong
~Someone *Refuses* Their Role
~Someone *Disagrees* With #Goal
~Someone Is *Untaught* In #Honor.©
#drMM

TW82 I Know Your #Wisdom...
...When I Know Who You #Honor.©
#drMM

TW83 #Energy Is Not Passion.
Energy Is...The *Power* To Move.

Passion Is...The *Purpose* For Moving.©
#drMM

TW84 FEELINGS...
If They Are Unimportant, Why Do We
Pursue...#Joy... #Love...#Peace..?©
#drMM

TW85 5 CIRCLES of #FRIENDS:
Those Who...
1) Need You
2) Feed You
3) Bleed You
4) Lead You
5) HEED You!©
#drMM

TW86 #LAW_of_RECOGNITION:
Everything You Want Is Already In Your
#Life... Merely Awaiting Your #Recognition of
It.©
#drMM

TW87 #PASSION...
What Are You Unwilling To Live Without..?©
#drMM

TW88 #ASSIGNMENT:
Those Who Unlock Your #Compassion...Are
Those To Whom You Are Assigned.©
#drMM

TW89 #CHANGE: When You *Want*
Something You Have Never Had...
You Must *Do* Something You Have Never
Done.©
#drMM

TW90 Your #FUTURE Has A Higher
Code of Conduct Than Your Present.©
#drMM

TW91 IF YOU FAIL...It Will Be Because
of Who You Chose To #Dishonor.
IF YOU #SUCCEED...It Will Be Because of
Who You Chose To #Honor.©
#drMM

TW92 1) The #Problem Nearest You...Is
The Secret Door To Your #Future.©
(David/Goliath)
2) #Problems...Are Invitations To
Significance.© #drMM

TW93   HONOR...Is The Seed That
Flourishes In *Every* #Environment Or
Season.
Honor *Creates* #Access...Before Genius/
Relationship.©
#drMM

TW94   Dominant Role of #Wisdom...
...Is To Recognize *Who* Qualifies For
HONOR.
When You Learn #Honor...
...You Have Learned *The Secret of Life.*©
#drMM

TW95   WORD To #POLITICIANS:
Your Willingness To Dishonor God Because
You #Fear Men...Is More
Dangerous Than The Men You Fear.©
#drMM

TW96   ANGER IS...
...#Seed For Change
...Birthplace For #Ideas
...Misdirected #Passion
...Clue To Your #Assignment.©
#drMM

TW97 #Problems...Make You Necessary To Others.
Problems...Make Others Necessary To You.©
#drMM

TW98 DESIRE...Is A Tyrant.
Make Each Desire...Your Child, *Waiting* For An *#Instruction. A Desire Is Not You, But Your #Servant.*©
#drMM

TW99 You Are Never Responsible For The #Pain of Those Who *Ignore* Your #Counsel.©
#drMM

TW100 Secrets of #Jesus:
Jesus Made No Attempt To Help Anyone... Who *Distrusted* Him.©
#drMM

TW101 CARING...Creates #Discerning.
Caring *Parent*...Discerns The Needs of A Child.
Caring *Employee*...Discerns The Needs of The *Organization.*©
#drMM

TW102 The Only Thing #God Owes You
Is... #OPPORTUNITY.
~To Learn
~To Serve
~To Repent
~To Obey
~To Change
~To Honor
~To Reach.©
#drMM

TW103 Only A #Fool *Ignores* The #Desires
of A King.©
#drMM

TW104 The Fragrance of #Honor...Is
Instant. (Jonathan)
The Odor of #Dishonor...Is *Eventual.*©
(Absalom)
#drMM

TW105 Your #Potential...Is Not A
#Prophecy of Your #Future.
Your Potential...Is Not Your #Destiny.
Your Potential...Is *Possibilities.*©
ie. Satan #drMM

TW106 YOUR #JOY... Reveals The *Quality* of Your #Decision_Making.©
#drMM

TW107 FEW WILL UNDERSTAND THIS...
Learning HOW To #Receive...Is As Important As #Giving.©
(Gift of #Access/Correction/Advice)
#drMM

TW108 #JOY...Is The Divine #Reward For Making A *Right* #Decision.©
#drMM

TW109 #QUEST:
What Is Your STRONGEST #Desire?
What Is The *Proof* It Is Important To You?
WHY Is It Important To You?
What Will It *Cost* You?
Will You *Pay* The Price?©
#drMM

TW110 #DIVORCE...Is Proof That First Impressions Don't Last.©
#drMM

TW111 WIFE:
When You Know A Man's Most Painful *Memories-*
You Will Understand His *#Decisions.*
When You Know His *#Fears-*
You Can Understand His *#Goals.*©
#drMM

TW112 YOUR #LIFE IS A PICTURE of:
...Your #Decisions
...#Mentor You Trusted
...What You MAGNIFY In Your #Mind
...Your CHOSEN #Focus.©
#drMM

TW113 MY 6 #DISCOMFORT ZONES:
1) #Time_Wasters
2) Meaningless #Conversation
3) The Deceptive
4) The Self-Obsessed
5) #Non_Learners
6) The Unthankful.©
#drMM

TW114 #PASTORAL_TALK:
Your #Future #Comfort Will Be Decided By

Who You Are Willing To #Train Today.©
#drMM

TW115 POISE...Is The Ability To #Discern The Ignorant Without Reacting To Them.©
#drMM

TW116 3 LIFE_CHANGERS FOR ME:
~Falling In Love With The_#Holy_Spirit
~Making 140 #Training_Videos For Staff
~Creating The_#Secret_Place For
The_#Holy_Spirit.©
#drMM

TW117 Whatever Is Missing In Your #Life, Is Something You Do Not Yet Value. Whatever You Are Attempting To Live Without, You Do Not Yet Value.©
#drMM

TW118 Some Use Their #Faith...To ENDURE Their Trial.
Some Use Their Faith...To ESCAPE Their Trial.
Choice Is *Yours*.© (Heb 11)
#drMM

TW119 #SUBMISSION...Without A #Reward Is A Mistake.©
(#Marriage. #Government. #Relationships.)
#drMM

TW120 #Law_of_Seed Cannot Be Over Taught; But WHAT...WHERE...WHY Is Important. Few Are Taught How To #Receive...From #God/Man.©
#drMM

TW121 #SINGLE_TALK:
~What Excites You Today...May *Bore* You
  Tomorrow.
~Does Their Presence *Improve* You?
~#Marriage *Bonds* You With Their
  #Weakness.©
#drMM

TW122 REWARDS of KNOWLEDGE...
~*Stops* Painful Losses/Experiences
~*Explains* Past #Failures
~*Creates* #Pleasures
~*Makes* #Success Easier/Quicker.©
#drMM

`TW123` EVERY #RELATIONSHIP...Has A Cost...Energy...Time...#Focus.
Sometimes, The Cost *Exceeds* The Pleasure.
EVERY #PLEASURE...Has A Price.©
#drMM

`TW124` WRITE YOUR OWN BOOK...
~Your Investment Will Verify Your #Caring Instead of Your #Bitterness.
~Your Labor Will Reveal Your #Passion/Not #Attitude.©
#drMM

`TW125` #PASTORAL_TALK:
Family...Your Desire To Give/Sow Is Not My #1 Concern. Your Skill At #Receiving Disturbs Me. You MUST Master RECEIVING...FIRST.©
#drMM

`TW126` #PAIN...Is How We #Discern What Is Most Important To Us.©
(Emotional Emptiness. Loneliness. Physical.)
#drMM

TW127 FOR NON-TITHERS ONLY: Distrusting #God...Will Be The *Costliest* #Decision of Your Lifetime.©
#drMM

TW128 Every #Environment...Has A Code of Conduct For *Entering* Or *Remaining* In It.© (#Beauty Made Esther Queen; #Obedience KEPT Her Queen.)
#drMM

TW129 FAVOR...Is Neither A #Miracle Nor Mystery.
FAVOR...Is A *Reward* For Pleasing Someone.©
(Pleasure...Favor...#Honor...#Prosperity)
#drMM

TW130 STOP Discussing...What You Want Others To #Forget.©
#drMM

TW131 #SILENCE...Is The #Seed For Misunderstanding.©
#Conflict...Is Caused By A Missing #Conversation.© #drMM

TW132 Someone's #Future Cannot Begin...
Until YOU Enter Their Life.©
Find Them.
(Jesus-Samaritan Woman/Elijah-Widow/
1 Kings 17)
#drMM

TW133 HURRY...Is The #Seed For *Regret*.
DELAY...Is The Seed For Your
Replacement.©
#drMM

TW134 YOUR ATTENTION...Decides The
Influence of Your #Critics.
Those Who Keep Your Attention...Have
Become Your Master.©
#drMM

TW135 PATIENCE...Is Often The
Explanation For *Delaying* A #Decision.©
#drMM

TW136 64 Years Old...Where Will I #Invest
My Life Next?
...In Those Who #Honor
...In Those Who *Pursue*

...In Those Who *Change.*©
#drMM

TW137 3 #PEOPLE YOU MUST NEVER CORRECT:
1) Someone You Don't #Love
2) Someone Who Won't Listen
3) Someone Not Under Your #Authority.©
#drMM

TW138 IF #GOD MADE YOU...The Way You Are...Why Would You Try To *Improve* Yourself? Fact: God Made You The Way You Were; You BECAME What You Are.©
#drMM

TW139 MY GREATEST #MISTAKES:
1) Trusting Untested
2) Not Firing The #Lazy
3) Giving Instructions Twice
4) Being #Sugar_Daddy To Sugar-Talkers.©
#drMM

TW140 #PASTORAL_TALK:
Those Unwilling To Come Hear You Teach...Disqualify Themselves For

Private #Counseling.©
#drMM

TW141 #SINGLE_TALK:
~Those Who Are Interesting...Are Not
  Always *Interested.*
~Those Who Are Interested...Are Not
  Always *Interesting.*©
#drMM

TW142 #SINGLE_MAN CKLIST:
1) Is She An Occasional #Liar?
2) Does Her HISTORY Inspire Your #Trust?
3) Is She Excited About YOUR #Dreams?©
#drMM

TW143 #SINGLE_MAN HEART GUARD:
~What Is She NOT Saying?
~What Is "The Bait" In This Fishing
  Experience?
~Is She Interesting Or Are You Just Bored?©
#drMM

TW144 The Sound of #Honor...Makes
Every *Other* Sound Unbearable.
The #Environment of Honor...#*Heals.*©
#drMM

TW145 #Humor Often *Hides* #Pain...But It Rarely *Heals* It.©
#drMM

TW146 Distance...Makes The #Heart *Wander.*©
#drMM

TW147 YOUR #IGNORANCE:
...Is The Only *Weapon* #Satan Has.
...The Only #*Problem* You Face.
...Is More *Destructive* Than #Demons.
...*Can* Be Cured.©
#drMM

TW148 Your Next #Season...Is Only ONE Person Away.©
(Eleazar...Rebekkah...Isaac)
(Ruth...Naomi...Boaz)
(David...Goliath...Kingship)
#drMM

TW149 RECEIVING... Is Taught In The Word of God Much More Than #Giving.©
Christ/Mercy/Healing/Instruction.
To Those Who RECEIVED...He GAVE.

(John 1:12)
#drMM

TW150 MASTER #RECEIVING..!
~#Instructions
~#Opportunities
~#Invitations
~#Differences
~#Correction
~#Advice
~#Change
~#Mentorship©
#drMM

TW151 CONFUSION...Is *Proof* A
#Deceiver Is *Present.*©
#drMM

TW152 What You Are Willing To Walk
Away From...Determines What #God Will
Bring To You.© (Ruth Left Moab/Met Boaz)
#drMM

TW153 Your #Seed...Shows What YOU
Can Do/Give.
Your #Harvest...Shows What GOD Can

Do/Give.
#Receiving...Is As Important As #Giving.©
#drMM

TW154 REJECTION..?
May You Never Have Anyone #GOD Did
Not Give You.©
#drMM

TW155 When #Wrong People Leave Your
Life...Wrong Things *Stop* Happening.©
(Jonah Overboard-Storm Stopped)
#drMM

TW156 Those Who Cannot Feel Your #Pain
Will Never Understand Your #Goals.
Those Who Disagree With Your *Goals* Will
Never Agree With Your *#Decisions.*©
#drMM

TW157 #Satan's Favorite Entry Point Will
Always Be Through...Someone *Close* To
You.©
(David/Absalom...Jesus/Judas)
#drMM

TW158 #SINGLE_TALK:
A #Fool Is Someone Who Makes The Same #Mistakes *Repeatedly.*© (Prov 26:11)
#drMM

TW159 Conduct You Permit...Is Conduct You *Approve.*©
#drMM

TW160 All #Men Fall...The Great Ones Get Back Up.©
#drMM

TW161 I Have Found More #Strength In Being Right...Than In Being Approved.©
#drMM

TW162 My ONLY #Assignment…Is To #Love.
Because I Love...
I #Teach...Write...#Mentor...Warn...
via TV/Internet/Books/Church...©
#drMM

TW163 YOUR ATTENTION...Will Always Be Toward Your Place of #Pain; The Person

Who Always Responds To That Will Become
Important To You.©
#drMM

TW164 REWARDS of #PAIN:
~Unlocks The Willingness To Listen.
~Reveals Who Cares *Most* About You.
~Makes You Willing To Reach.©
#drMM

TW165 PLANNING...Makes Your #Future
Gloriously Predictable.©
#drMM

TW166 #SINGLE_TALK:
A #Kiss Is Not A #Relationship.
Neither...Is A Meal Or #Conversation.©
#drMM

TW167 YOUR #DESIRES...Are Not
#Prophecies.©
#drMM

TW168 MENTORSHIP:
You Cannot #Mentor Anyone...Who Doesn't
Admire You.

You Cannot #Learn...From Anyone You Resent.©
#drMM

TW169 What You Can Walk Away From...
You Have Mastered.
What You Cannot Walk Away From...Has Mastered You.©
(Samson/ Joseph)
#drMM

TW170 Some Are Running...*From* Their #PAST.
Some Are Running...*Toward* Their #FUTURE.©
#drMM

TW171 True #Friends...Have The *Same* #Enemies.©
#drMM

TW172 Friends Create...#*Comfort*.
#Enemies Create...#*Rewards*.©
#drMM

TW173 God Gave YOU A #Family...To

Prepare You For Your #Enemies.
Everything In Your Future...Is *Already* At
Your House.©
(Judas/Absalom)
#drMM

TW174 Any Movement Towards #ORDER...
Creates *Instant* #Pleasure.©
#drMM

TW175 HOW TO KNOW YOUR
#ASSIGNMENT:
~Whose #Pain Do You *Feel?*
~Whose #Enemies Do You *Confront?*
~Who Do You Long To *Protect?*©
#drMM

TW176 3 THINGS I WANT IN EVERY
ROOM I ENTER:
1) Light
2) Movement
3) Sound©
#drMM

TW177 If Everyone Is Treated EQUAL...
How Do You Reward #Loyalty?

Competence? #Passion? Determination? #Faithfulness?©
#drMM

TW178 WHATEVER IS MISSING IN YOUR #LIFE...Is Something You Do Not Yet Know *How* To #Receive.©
(John 1:12)
#drMM

TW179 God Talks To *Families*...Through Their *Children*.
God #Talks To *Nations*...Through Their #*Economy*.©
#drMM

TW180 INGRATITUDE...Is The *First* Step Toward #Loss.
(Loss of #Access To A Leader...Loss of Job... Favor.)©
#drMM

TW181 Attack Is Proof...#Satan Just Discovered Your #Future.©
#drMM

`TW182` 7 #REACTIONS THAT REVEAL #CHARACTER:
Your Reaction To...
~#Authority
~#Correction
~#Gifts
~#Greatness
~#Opportunity
~#Debt
~#Injustice©
#drMM

`TW183` FAVORITES:
Verse: Isa 43:2
Chapter: Ps 119
Book: 1,001 Wisdom Keys of Mike Murdock
Food: Chinese
Author: Sidney Sheldon
Conversationalist: Deborah Murdock Johnson©
#drMM

`TW184` Integrity...Makes Inferiority *Impossible.*©
#drMM

`TW185` DISHONOR....Is An Explanation...

of #Character, #Prejudice And Perception.©
#drMM

TW186 DISRESPECT...Is The #Seed For #Loss. (Loss of *Access*...Influence...Job... #Credibility)©
#drMM

TW187 A WOMAN...Finds It Difficult To Follow A Man She Is Able To #Deceive.©
#drMM

TW188 7 THINGS A WOMAN SHOULD KNOW ABOUT HER MAN...His:
1) #History
2) #Weakness
3) #Pain
4) #Heroes
5) #Money Philosophy
6) #Who He Honors
7) #Fear_of_God©
#drMM

TW189 WHAT IS #DESTINY..?
Simply..."The Outcome of Your #Decisions."©
#drMM

TW190 #UNITY...Is Decided By ONE.©
#drMM

TW191 Men Do Not #Marry A Woman Because of Her #Beauty; They Marry A Woman Because of How They *Feel* In Her Presence.©
#drMM

TW192 THINK TWICE BEFORE #MARRIAGE:
~If They Are *Uncomfortable* In The Presence of #God.
~If They *Never* Ask Quality #Questions About Your #Assignment.©
#drMM

TW193 NOBODY IS EQUAL...
#IQ/Discerning/Skills/#Wisdom/#Opportunity.
#SOW...Into Those With *Less.*
#LEARN...From Those With *More.*©
#drMM

TW194 #Beauty Is Always Pursued; So Beauty Rarely #Learns How To *Reach.*©
#drMM

`TW195` #Beauty Is Served First; So Beauty Rarely Learns To #*Serve.*©
#drMM

`TW196` #Beauty Is Admired; So Beauty Rarely Learns To #*Admire.*©
#drMM

`TW197` What You #Fail To #Conquer Will *Eventually* Conquer You.
(#Anger...#Depression...#Bitterness...#Fear...)©
#drMM

`TW198` NOBODY...Is As They *First* Appear.©
#drMM

`TW199` #SINGLE_TALK:
~How Did They Exit Their Last #Relationship?
~Is #Conversation Burdensome?
~Is Their "Hunger" For Attention?/God?/Aid?© #drMM

`TW200` SOUNDS IN CONVERSATIONS:
~Envy?
~Hints For Aid?

~Kindness?
~Hunger For Attention?
~#Control?
~#Joy?
~Concern?
~#Servanthood?
~#Self_Love?©
#drMM

TW201 Your Reaction To My #Problem...Is A *Picture* of Your #Heart.©
#drMM

TW202 The Proof of Repentance...Is Reimbursement.©
(Zaccheus Paid Back 4 Times What He Took.) #drMM

TW203 Every #Conversation Contains A #Giver...And A #Receiver.©
#drMM

TW204 The Burden of Adaptation...Is *Always* On The Pursuer.©
#drMM

TW205 Every #Moment Contains A #Difference; The #Wise *Find* It.©
#drMM

TW206 What You #Respect...Will Move *Toward* You.©
(God...#Miracles...Wisdom...#Finances... People)
#drMM

TW207 3 WORDS CHANGED MY LIFE: Health Crisis/4 Hrs Daily Prayer.
The_#Holy_Spirit Spoke: "Decisions Decide Wealth."©
Revolutionary.
#drMM

TW208 THE RAREST THING ON EARTH...Is Someone Who *Really* Cares.©
#drMM

TW209 THE UNEXPLORED...Will Forever Be Unknown.
~A #Relationship
~A #Conversation
~An Experience© #drMM

TW210 PREJUDICE...Is A Thief...of #Pleasure, Change And New.©
(Whether Against Race/Gender/Wealth/Religion)
#drMM

TW211 Your Past Only Happened Once; Your #Memory Has Kept It Alive.©
#drMM

TW212 Your #Words To Me...Explain How You *See* Me.©
#drMM

TW213 What You Make Happen For Others...#God Will Make Happen For You.©
(Eph 6:8)
(Spirit Spoke This/2:30a On 5 Day Fast/My Motto)
#drMM

TW214 Today I Will Reap My #Harvest... From My Yesterday #Seed..!©
#drMM

TW215 Whatever You Keep Loving...

Eventually #Rewards You.©
(Boxing/M Ali...Basketball/M Jordan)
#drMM

TW216 GOALS:
Your Goals Choose...Your #*Mentors.*
Your Goals Choose...What You #*Conquer.*
Your Goals Choose...What You #*Learn.*©
#drMM

TW217 Yes...Prison Is A Part of Life,
Too...For Those Who Cannot Suppress Or
Direct Their #Anger *Appropriately.*©
#drMM

TW218 The Difference In Men...Is Revealed
By The Kind of Women They *Want* To
Impress.©
#drMM

TW219 If You Cannot Be Trusted With...
An Instruction...
You Will Not Be Entrusted With...Your
Future.©
#drMM

TW220 WRONG PEOPLE...Never Leave Your Life *Voluntarily.*©
(Absalom/Delilah/Haman/Korah/Jonah)
#drMM

TW221 #Submission Is...The Transference of Responsibility To Another.©
#drMM

TW222 #SILENCE Is...A Control Weapon, A Favorite Among *#Deceivers.*©
#drMM

TW223 #Absence Is...The #Seed for Disorder.©
(Leader Away From His People/Moses)
(Father Away From Home)
#drMM

TW224 #DISINTEREST...Is The Signal To Exit.©
(Jesus - Shake Dust Off Your Feet)
#drMM

TW225 NEVER STAY...Where There Is The Absence of #Favor.© #drMM

www.twitter.com/DrMikeMurdock

TW226 The #Problem You Can Solve... Determines Who Pursues You.©
#drMM

TW227 #BITTERNESS...Is *Deadlier* Than #Injustice.©
#drMM

TW228 THE MASTER SECRET TO #SUCCESS...Is Simply *Knowing* Who To Please.©
(Joseph/Daniel/Ruth/Esther/Jesus)
#drMM

TW229 #LONELINESS...Is When You Feel *Unimportant* To Someone Who Is Important To You.©
#drMM

TW230 IF EVERYONE IS EQUAL...Who Will You *Learn* From?©
#drMM

TW231 IF YOU WERE YOUR #ENEMY... How Would You *Destroy* You?©
#drMM

TW232 Your #Goals-Decide What You *Need* To Learn.
Your #Humility-Decides How *Quickly* You Will Learn It.
Your #Passion-Decides *Price* You Will Pay.©
#drMM

TW233 *Honor* Is...Attitude Toward *Another.*
#*Humility* Is...Attitude Toward *Yourself.*©
#drMM

TW234 Sometimes, You Don't Need An Ocean; A *Single* Swallow Often Satisfies.©
#drMM

TW235 THE_#SECRET_PLACE:
The More I Discuss With The_#Holy_Spirit.
The *Less* I Discuss With People.©
#drMM

TW236 Your #HEALING...Is God's Responsibility.
Your #HEALTH...Is YOUR Responsibility.©
#drMM

TW237 YOUR #CRITICISM...of Others Will *Diminish* Your #Influence On Them.©
#drMM

TW238 #God Often Hides His Greatest Gifts In His Most *Flawed* Vessels...So Only The Most *#Passionate* Can Discover Them.©
#drMM

TW239 #INGRATITUDE...*Stops* #Favor.©
#drMM

TW240 You Cannot *Earn* In A Lifetime... What #Favor Can *Give* You In A Day.©
#drMM

TW241 A HIDDEN #GIFT FROM GOD... Has Arrived Near You...Unopened... Unexperienced. Unenjoyed.
You Have Not Recognized It.
Yet.© #drMM

TW242 When You *Prepare* For #Failure...It Will *Find* You.©
#drMM

TW243 When You Don't Like A Feeling...
Replace It.©
#drMM

TW244 God Loves...N-E-W.
Even His #Mercies Are NEW.
EVERY Morning.
Forget Former Things...I Will Do A NEW
Thing.
Get #ADDICTED To It.©
#drMM

TW245 #PROTÉGÉ_TALK:
TV News...Is "Their" World. Not Yours.
Your Immediate #Focus...Is YOUR World.
World Is Menu of Ingredients. You Create
Meal.©
#drMM

TW246 God Gave You A #Mind...To *Resize*
Your #Experiences.©
#drMM

TW247 Make TOMORROW So Big...
Yesterday *Dies.*©
#drMM

TW248 4 REASONS For
#CONFRONTATION:
~Attempt To *Preserve* A #Relationship
~*Remove* Confusion
~*Prevent* A Tragedy
~*Establish* Order©
#drMM

TW249 CREATE #SUCCESS RITUALS...
~7 Minutes In The_#Secret_Place
~Read 1 Prov A Day
~Prophecy To Your Day
~Read Thanksgiving List A-Z©
#drMM

TW250 I PROPHECY...YOUR DAY..!
For NEW Things..!
New Ideas...
New Streams of Honor
New #Hope
New Strategies
New Connections©
#drMM

TW251 Stop Creating...*More* Than You Can
Manage.© #drMM

TW252 TIRED EYES...*Rarely* See A Good #Future.©
#drMM

TW253 #ANGER...Is A #Signpost To A #Problem God Wants You To *Solve.*©
#drMM

TW254 #FAITH...
Faith Is...Confidence In God.
Faith Comes...When You HEAR Something God Would Say.
Faith Decides...Divine #Favor.©
#drMM

TW255 #SEED...Is Powerless...Until It Enters Soil.
Seed/Soil Creates The Covenant of Two That Breaks Concrete Sidewalks Into Pieces.©
#drMM

TW256 DISCOMFORT...Is The School for #Poise.©
#drMM

TW257 When I Know Who Likes You...I Can Predict Your #Future.©
(Ruth/Boaz...David/Abigail...Joseph/Pharoah)
#drMM

TW258 FAILURE CKLIST:
1) #Disobedient Toward Parents
2) Defiant Toward Police
3) Resentful of The Rich
4) Believes In #Luck©
#drMM

TW259 You Will Always Act Like The Person You *Think* You Are.©
#drMM

TW260 PURSUIT...Is The True Proof of #Desire.©
(Relationships...#Prosperity...Mentorship...#Romance)
#drMM

TW261 What You Repeatedly Hear...You *Eventually* #Believe.©
#drMM

TW262 Parasites Want...Attention;
#Protégés Want...#Mentorship.
Parasites Want...A Cheerleader;
Protégés Want...A Coach.©
#drMM

TW263 IF #MONEY IS EVIL...Why Hasn't
Satan *Doubled* Your Income *Weekly?*©
(Satan Did Not Double Job's Income.)
#drMM

TW264 Someone Is *Always* Observing You...
Who Is Capable of *Greatly* Blessing You.©
(Boaz & Ruth...Rebekkah & Eleazar)
#drMM

TW265 Bad Times...Bring Good People
Together.
One of Great Benefits of Present Economy
Crisis...Is *Trustworthy* #Friendships.©
#drMM

TW266 SELF-ABSORPTION...Is The Enemy
of #Relationship.
Not Mere #Attitude; It Is A Philosophy
Toward Life.

#Self_Worship.©
#drMM

TW267 #PRESENCE...Changes The Equation of *Every* #Environment.
When The Rebel Is Removed,The Storm Will Cease.© (Jonah)
#drMM

TW268 #ENVIRONMENT...Does Not Change The Nature of A #Fool.©
#drMM

TW269 The #Recognition of #Greatness... *Confirms* Your Own Greatness.©
#drMM

TW270 Never Doubt The #Future of The Man...Who *#Honors* Greatness.©
#drMM

TW271 THE UNDISCERNING...Will *Always* Consider You Unimportant.©
#drMM

TW272 #LYING...Is A *Chosen* Affliction.©
#drMM

TW273 TWO KINDS/MINISTRY:
Focus On...
~#RECEIVING *From* God
  (Forgiveness Etc.) Or
~#Giving *To* God
  (Offerings Etc.)
Both Are Needed.©
#drMM

TW274 If Your Entire #Harvest Happens
Here...#Heaven Is *Unnecessary.*©
#drMM

TW275 #THINKING...Is Simply
Emotional Jogging.©
#drMM

TW276 #LEADERSHIP_TALK
The Unhappy Follower...Has Not Yet
Discerned The #Wisdom of The #Leader.©
#drMM

TW277 DISCRETION...
The *Smaller* The Small-Print...The *Bigger*
The Headline.©
#drMM

TW278 #PASTORAL_TALK:
The Unhappy Follower...Usually Has A
Different Destination.©
#drMM

TW279 UNREST...Occurs When Your
Spirit Has Discerned Information That Your
#Mind Has Not Yet Reported.©
#drMM

TW280 A Word To SONGWRITERS:
Caution...*Suffocates* #Creativity.©
#drMM

TW281 HOW TO CHANGE A MAN:
1) *Timing*~Esther
2) *#Questions*~Queen of Sheba
3) *Directness*~Ruth
4) *#Credibility*~Naaman's Maid
5) *#Honor*~Abigail©
#drMM

TW282 TO PROTÉGÉS:
NEWS...Avoid #Problem_Zones Where You
Have No Authority.

#FOOLS...Compassion Does Not Change Them.©
#drMM

TW283 #WISDOM...Is Knowing The Divine #Reaction To A Human #Problem.©
#drMM

TW284 YOUR #QUEST Decides...
~*What* You See
~*Who* Sees You
~What You *Overcome*
~What You *Ignore*
~The *Changes* You Make©
#drMM

TW285 #SINGLE_TALK:
Interest...Is Not Proof of #Love.©
(The Lion Is Interested In The Antelope...
Cat Chases Mouse)
#drMM

TW286 WOMEN:
Immerse Yourself In His World (Esther).
Prove #Trustworthiness To Those He Trusts (Ruth).

www.twitter.com/DrMikeMurdock

Don't Resent How He Uses His #Time
(Prov 31).©
#drMM

`TW287` NO #WOMAN...Can Follow The
#Man Who Refuses To Lead.©
#drMM

`TW288` NO #MAN...Can Protect The
#Woman Who Refuses To Follow.©
#drMM

`TW289` #LAZINESS...Is *Silent* Defiance.©
#drMM

`TW290` #HONOR...Has A Fragrance *Instantly*
Discernable.©
#drMM

`TW291` #SINGLE_TALK:
#Desire...Is Neither An Instruction Nor A
Prophecy.©
#drMM

`TW292` DATING QUESTIONS:
Is Meaningful Talk A Struggle?

Do They Energize You, Or You Just Lonely?
Do #Questions Show True Interest In Your
#Passion?©
#drMM

TW293 #DATING:
~How Do They Improve Me?
~What Secret Fears Are Emerging?
~Do They Show Honor? Dishonor?
~Do I Feel Need For Caution?©
#drMM

TW294 #SINGLE_TALK:
~In What Scenario Would They Embarrass
  Me?
~In a Crisis, Could They #Pray Effectively
  For Me?
~Are They Successful Or Needy?©
#drMM

TW295 SINGLE-SOUNDS:
Self-Absorbed Or *Servant's* #Heart?
Comforting Or *Corrective?*
Victim-Talk Or *Victorious?*
Respectful Or *Retaliator?*©
#drMM

TW296 #DATING:
What Interest Do They Show In MY Problems?
Do I Have Desire To Discuss My #QUEST With Them?
Do They *Lie, #Slither* Or Avoid?©
#drMM

TW297 Never Give More #Time To A *Critic* Than You Would Give To A *#Friend.*©
#drMM

TW298 DATE_ZONE:
Those Who Love Your Energy...May *Resent* Your #Goals.
Those Who Love To LOOK At You...May Not Want To LISTEN To You.©
#drMM

TW299 SOMEWHERE...SOMEONE...Is Out of Place...Because Their Place Is *Next* To You.©
#drMM

TW300 6-Basics: #HONOR Parents/God/

#Boss At Highest Level. Examine All #Favor/Open Doors. Get Close To A $$Mentor/Listen To The_#Holy_Spirit.©
#drMM

TW301 HONOR...Creates #Access Into *Any* #Environment.
HONOR...Will Advance You *Faster* Than Genius.
HONOR...Flourishes In *Every* #Season.©
#drMM

TW302 EVERY WORSHIPPER...Is A *Secret* #Warrior.©
#drMM

TW303 Every #Thinking Man *Craves* Improvement. #Wife...Must Know What He Wants To Improve...©
#drMM

TW304 #SINGLE_TALK...
Players...Are Not Prayers.
#Prayers...Are Not Players.©
#drMM

TW305 A #WOMAN...*Stops* Admiring The Man She Can #Deceive.©
#drMM

TW306 #PASTORAL_TALK:
Stop Teaching Those Who Stop Listening.©
(Jesus/Pharisees)
#drMM

TW307 #DESTINY...Is Simply Wherever Your #Decisions Bring You.©
#drMM

TW308 #MAN_TALK:
The *Beauty* of A Snake Does Not *Remove* Its Poison...Nor *Diminish* Its Danger.©
#drMM

TW309 What Part of You Is...*Broken?*
Does It Matter To You?
What Will Happen...If You Don't #Change?
Have You Tried...*#God?*©
#drMM

TW310 Every #Friendship...Has A *Price.*
Every Friendship...Has #*Expectations.*

Every Friendship...Can *#Change.*©
#drMM

TW311 #SINGLE_TALK:
Don't Walk Through A Door...Until You Are
Invited.©
#drMM

TW312 YOUR #LIFE QUEST...
~What Is It?
~Is It Scriptural?
~What Will It Cost You?
~What Will You Do Differently-To *Obtain*
  It?©
#drMM

TW313 Every #Conversation...Needs A
#Healer.©
#drMM

TW314 5 CIRCLES of #LIFE:
~Circle of *#Caring*
~Circle of *#Correction*
~Circle of *#Counsel*
~Circle of *#Comfort*
~Circle of *#Conversation*© #drMM

TW315 DIFFERENCE IN SEASONS IS:
~A Person
~A Decision
~What You'll Stop Doing
~Who Likes You
~Voice You #Trust
~Who You #Honor©
#drMM

TW316 No #Fool...Stays Hidden.©
#drMM

TW317 #WISDOM...Is The Ability To
Anticipate The #Consequences of A
#Decision.©
#drMM

TW318 ONE WRONG PERSON...Can
Become A *Lifetime* Heartache.©
#drMM

TW319 The #Anointing You #*Respect* Is
The Anointing You *Attract*.©
#drMM

TW320 #SINGLE_TALK:
The Cure For Ingratitude Is...*Loss.*©
#drMM

TW321 #SUBMISSION...Is Not Ownership.
Submission...Is *Permission* To Protect.©
#drMM

TW322 #PASTORAL_TALK:
One True Protégé Is Worth 1,000 Pharisees.
We Teach The Masses To Find The Protégé.©
#drMM

TW323 #PATIENCE...Is Simply Waiting
For Your #Enemy To Make His *Next*
Mistake.©
#drMM

TW324 #SINGLE_TALK:
Do You Really Want A #Mate Too Dumb To
Discern You..?©
#drMM

TW325 #SINGLE_TALK:
Their *Behavior* Towards You Reveals Their
Perception of You.© Duh.!! #drMM

TW326 #SINGLE_TALK:
You Don't Need Someone To Make You
#Happy;
You Need Someone Who Won't Make You
Sad.©
#drMM

TW327 To Be Unforgotten...You Must Do
Something Unforgettable.©
#drMM

TW328 THE_#SECRET_PLACE...
...Is Not Where You Give Instructions *To*
God;
...It Is Where You RECEIVE Instructions
From God.©
#drMM

TW329 PROBLEM:
What #Instruction Was Dishonored?
What Is Biblical Solution?
Who Was Wronged?
What Will Stop It From Reoccurring?©
#drMM

TW330 ABORTION:

America's Unwillingness To Listen...Does
Not Remove Our Responsibility To Warn.©
#drMM

TW331 AUTHORITY...Is Only Legitimate
If It...
~*Protects* You From #Enemies
~*Provides* for You, Your #Family
~*Promotes* #Peace©
#drMM

TW332 #ADMIRATION...Is The #Seed For
#*Relationship.*©
#drMM

TW333 APPROVAL:
Stay Thankful...When You Are *Receiving*
Approval.
Stay Thoughtful...When You Are *Giving*
Approval.©
#drMM

TW334 ADVICE FROM JONAH:
Sometimes Even A Good Man...Does Not
Belong With You.
Even Good Men Are *Out* of Place.© #drMM

TW335 Good People In *Wrong* Places...Are
A *Bad* Experience.©
(Advice From Jonah On Ship With Sailors
Who Threw Jonah Off Ship)
#drMM

TW336 Men of God...Know Where They
Don't Belong.©
(The Jonah-Seminar)
#drMM

TW337 It Is EASY To Distinguish Your
#Imagination From The_#Holy_Spirit;
The Spirit *Never* Produces #Confusion, Nor
#Worry.©
#drMM

TW338 Good Men In *Wrong* Places...
Create *Stormy* Experiences.©
(Jonah-Talks To #Singles/The Boat)
#drMM

TW339 Twitter Is...*Access.*
#Access...Is #*Favor.*
Favor...Can Be Lost As *Quickly*
As It Was Given.

Block...#Fools. *All* of Them.©
#drMM

TW340 "TWITTER"...*Kills* Pride.
You Discover That God Has Been Talking To
Others...*Behind Your Back..!*©
#drMM

TW341 The World You Are *Experiencing*...
Is The World YOU *Created* For Yourself.©
(Thru Decisions-Focus-Faith-Doubt-
Attitude)
#drMM

TW342 RIGHT #WORDS...Can *Change*
Consequences.©
(ie. #Repentance of Thief On Cross/Nineveh)
#drMM

TW343 Many Who Want To *Please* You...
Don't Want To #*Listen* To You.©
(Crazy, Isn't It..!?)
#drMM

TW344 A Good #*Experience*...Is Not A
Prediction of A Good #*Relationship.*© #drMM

TW345 THINK ON THIS...
Most People...Want You Pleased;
Few People...Want To Please You.©
#drMM

TW346 Admiration...Is The Seed For
Access.©
(Zaccheus/Jesus...Pharaoh/Joseph)
#drMM

TW347 YOUR LIFE...Is Whatever You
Decide Is Important.©
Please Think On This. It Is Explosive. Your
#Family? $$? An Offense?
#drMM

TW348 WHOEVER You Keep
#Criticizing...Will Eventually Quit
#Listening To You—Their Survival Depends
On It.©
#drMM

TW349 JEALOUSY...Is The #*Fear* of Being
Unimportant To Someone Important To You.©
#drMM

TW350 WAR...Is Always Between Two Men.©
(Nations Don't Know Each Other Enough To #Hate. Have You Ever...Ever...*Hated* A Nation?)
#drMM

TW351 YOUR SUCCESS...Is Determined By What You Are Willing To *Ignore.*©
(An Offense/Failure/#Rejection...Etc.)
#drMM

TW352 MY #ADDICTIONS:
1. Presence of God
2. #Books
3. Meaningful #Conversation
4. Gentleness
5. Scalp Massage
6. #Learning
7. Waterfalls©
#drMM

TW353 THE MOST Heartbreaking Person In Your #Life Is...Someone You *Cannot* Impress.©

(Whatever You Do, Respond To Those You #Love.)
#drMM

TW354 MY 2 GREATEST #FEARS:
1. Fear of #Believing A Lie (Deception).
2. Fear of Not Fully Understanding...How To #LOVE.©
#drMM

TW355 #JOY IS ALWAYS...Just *One* Feeling Away.©
#drMM

TW356 #PRAYER:
THOUGHTS...Are Not Prayers.
NEEDS...Are Not Prayers.
#WORRY...Is Not A Prayer.
DISCUSSIONS...Are Not Prayers.
Think.©
#drMM

TW357 #CHANGE...Is *One* Decision Away.
Change...Your #*Quest*.
Change...Your *Focus*.
Change...What You *Study*.

Change...Your #Words / Tone.©
#drMM

TW358 TWO PHILOSOPHIES:
1. #Self_Worship
2. #Servanthood©
(Discern Your #Friends & You Can Predict
The #Future of Your Relationship)
#drMM

TW359 INVENTORY 4 INVESTMENTS:
1) Thoughts
2) #Time
3) Energy
4) #Words
Then...
Never Invest...In An #Enemy.©
#drMM

TW360 Divine Replacements...Are Always
An Improvement.
#Singles...Relationships
Career...Your Job©
#drMM

TW361 3 Greatest #Mistakes Women Make:

~That All #Men Are The Same
~That Criticizing A Man Makes You
  Interesting
~That #Attention Is Admiration©
#drMM

TW362 Comfort...The *Feeble*
Lift...The *Fallen*
#Listen...To The *Wise*
#Believe...The *Proven*
#Teach...*Protégés*
Identify...*Enemies*
Note...*Fools*©
#drMM

TW363 #PASTORAL_TALK:
Lesson #1 In Teaching
...Not Everyone Is *Ready.*©
#drMM

TW364 YOUR #FUTURE...Will Require
More #Preparation Than Your Present.©
#drMM

TW365 #SINGLE_TALK:
Never #Marry Someone...Who Doesn't Treat

You Better Than You Would Treat Yourself.©
#drMM

TW366 3 PEOPLE YOU MUST #TEACH:
1) Those *Under* Your Authority.
2) Those Who *Ask* Appropriate #Questions.
3) Those Who *Admire* You.©
#drMM

TW367 Words That *Gratify* The #Wise...
Agitate The #Fool.©
#drMM

TW368 THE HELPFUL... Are Never *Out*
of Place.©
#drMM

TW369 EVERY #GIVER Is Searching For
The *Qualified*...To BLESS.©
#drMM

TW370 Never Perform...For An *Unhappy*
Audience.©
#drMM

TW371 You Don't Choose Who Motivates

You...You Discover Them.©
#drMM

TW372 #PROTÉGÉ_TALK:
The Passion That Motivates You To *#Learn*...
Does Not Necessarily Qualify You To *#Teach*.©
#drMM

TW373 Your Appearance Is A Sales
Presentation...of What You Want Me To Buy.©
#drMM

TW374 #SINGLE_TALK:
Do You *Really* Want A #Mate...Who Can't
Find You..??©
#drMM

TW375 3 Replaceable People In Your #Life:
1. The *#Scornful*
2. The *#Stalker*
3. The *#Silent*©
#drMM

TW376 #PROTÉGÉ_TALK:
I Have Never Had A *Happy* Relationship
With Someone Who *Doubted* My #Ability To

Hear God's Voice.©
#drMM

TW377 PRAYER For #PASTORS:
Father, Keep Us Focused/Bold/Kind...As We
Pour Your Healing #Wisdom Into *Wounded*
#Hearts of Our People Tomorrow.©
#drMM

TW378 AGREEMENT...Is When Two
People Have The *Same* Information.©
#drMM

TW379 Ignorance...Is When You Don't Know.
Stupid...Is When You Won't #*Listen* To Who
Does Know.©
#drMM

TW380 3 ASSASSINS:
Abortionists...Assassins of #Leaders in *Womb*
Critics...Assassins of #*Hope*
Absaloms...Assassins of Your #*Influence*©
#drMM

TW381 #PROTÉGÉ_TALK:
I Stop *Talking*...When You Stop #*Listening*.

I Stop *Teaching*...When You Stop *#H*

#drMM

TW382 3 PEOPLE YOU CANNOT HELP:
Anyone Who...
~Doesn't Think They Have A #Problem
~Thinks YOU Are Their Problem
~Lies To You©

#drMM

TW383 Father...Use Our Tweets
...To *#Heal*
...To *Energize*
...To *Re-Focus*
...To *Reveal*
...To Birth *#Hope*
#Honor *Every* Effort Today.©

#drMM

TW384 7 Tones That Stop Weddings:
~Argumentive
~Dismissive
~Scornful
~Corrective
~Accusatory
~#Disinterest

~Condescension©
#drMM

TW385 4 LIFE CHANGERS:
~Invest 1st 7 Minutes In The_#Secret_Place
  Every AM
~Create Dream-Wall
~Turn 1 Desire Into A...#Quest
~Ask #Questions©
#drMM

TW386 Everything #God Promised
Arrived... *Disguised* As An #Opportunity.©
#drMM

TW387 I Let Go of Anything That Stops Me.
I Let Go of Anything That Slows Me Down.
I Let Go of Anything That Breaks My
#Focus on You,
#Holy_Spirit, I Let Go!©
#drMM

TW388 The #Quality of My #Friends
Unleash Incredible Self-Confidence In My
Value.© #drMM

TW389 Protocol For The_#Holy_Spirit?
SINGING.
Did Not Know This Until 7-13-94.
Have Written 800 #Love Songs To Him...
SING! He Enters...
#drMM

TW390 DAY KEYS:
Dignify #Moments.
Sculpture #Environment.
Exude #Gratitude.
Lavish #Honor.
Embrace #Difference.
Question #Wisely.©
#drMM

TW391 #Happy Voices...Birth *Energy.*
Unhappy Voices...Birth *Ideas.*©
#drMM

TW392 LADIES...
The Fragrance of Your #*Words*
Will Be Remembered Longer Than
The Fragrance of *Perfume.*©
#drMM

TW393 Anything *Unpursued*...Will Be
Unexperienced.©
(The_#Holy_Spirit-#Healing-#Relationship Etc.)
#drMM

TW394 GOD...
What Part of #God Is Still Undiscovered By
You?
Have Your #Beliefs Enabled You To
Accomplish Your #Life Purpose?©
#drMM

TW395 #PROTÉGÉ_TALK:
Your #Harvest...Is Not A Picture of Your
Willingness To #Give.
Your Harvest...Is A #Picture of Your Ability
To #Receive.©
drMM

TW396 QUESTIONS:
How Are You Measuring Your Improvements?
What Small #Change Would Make A BIG
Difference?
When Will You Make IT?©
#drMM

TW397 #LEADERSHIP:
#Leaders...Do Not *Choose* Followers.
#Followers...Choose Leaders.©
#drMM

TW398 Everything You Want...Has A
Hidden Path To It.
The Path Is Called...*#Opportunity.*©
#drMM

TW399 YOUR #FEELINGS...Are Not YOU.
They Are Simply The Fragrance of Your
#Thoughts.©
(Sometimes Odor...Smile!)
#drMM

TW400 If You Have A Single Penny In The
Bank...
You Have Mastered The Willingness To
#Trust.©
#drMM

TW401 If My Presence Is A #Problem...I
Won't Repeat It.©
#drMM

TW402 #SINGLE_TALK:
If It Is Not Your True #QUEST...It Will
Never Be Your Experience.©
#drMM

TW403 #SINGLE_TALK:
#Adaptation...Is The Burden of The
Pursuer—Not The Pursued.©
#drMM

TW404 #SINGLE_TALK:
When I Know What You #LOVE...I Know
What You Require.©
#drMM

TW405 #SINGLE_TALK:
When I Understand What You *Require*...I
Understand My *Role* In Your #Life.©
#drMM

TW406 #SINGLE_TALK Humor:
#Marriage...Is Like Buying A *Restaurant*
When All You Really Wanted Was...A
Pancake.©
(Smile-Plz)
#drMM

www.twitter.com/DrMikeMurdock

TW407 #GOD_EXPERIENCE:
If You Met God And Did Not #Change...You
Did Not Meet God.©
#drMM

TW408 #SINGLE_TALK:
Whatever You Can Live Without...*You Will.*©
#drMM

TW409 Every #Problem Left Unresolved...
Is Because A #Scripture Is Not Believed.©
#drMM

TW410 When I Hear Your *Music,* I Know
How You #*Feel.*
When I Hear You #Talk, I Know Who You
Honor.
When I See Your #*Friends,* I Know Who You
#*Trust.*©
#drMM

TW411 *Distrusting* The *Right* Person...Is
Far Costlier Than #*Trusting* The *Wrong*
Person.©
#drMM

TW412 The #Wrong Voice...Is Not The Trap.
Ignoring The Right Voice...Is The Trap.©
(Adam/God...Samson/Manoah)
#drMM

TW413 #POLITICS:
Dishonoring Our #President...May Be
Deadlier Than Any #Mistake He May
Make.©
(Be Careful W/Weapon of #Disrespect)
#drMM

TW414 #SINGLE_TALK:
Think Twice Before #Marriage...If He Has
Not Established A History of #Honor.©
(Authority-Parents-You-#God)
#drMM

TW415 #RELATIONSHIPS:
#Marriage...Is A Covenant of *Consequences.*©
(You #Marry Their #History And The Divine
Consequences To It.)
#drMM

TW416 #SINGLE_TALK:
If You *Take* Something #God Did *Not* Give

You...He Will Take *Back* Something He *Gave* You.©
(Adam/Tree...David/Bathsheba)
#drMM

TW417 #SINGLE_TALK:
The *Greater* The #Honor...The *Longer* The #Romance.©
#drMM

TW418 #MOMENTS:
A MOMENT Should Be Sipped...Before Being *Swallowed*.©
#drMM

TW419 #SEED_TALK:
#Conversation...Is The #Seed For #*Understanding*.©
#drMM

TW420 #ART_of_RECEIVING:
Receiving...Is Very Important Because It Will Birth Your Ability To #Give.©
(From God/People~#Love, Etc.)
#drMM

TW421 #HONOR:
Honor *Flourishes*...In Every *Season*.
Honor Succeeds...In Every *#Environment*.
Honor Opens *Doors*...*#Genius* Cannot.©
#drMM

TW422 #PROTÉGÉ_TALK:
Think On Your Next...#Life_Quest.
What Is Worthy of...TOTAL #Focus?
#Ministry? Mentorship? #Mate?
QUEST? Obsession?©
#drMM

TW423 IMAGINE...What You Could Gain By...
~Total #FOCUS On Your Quest
~Apologizing
~Asking More #Questions
~Exuding #Gratitude©
#drMM

TW424 #LOVE:
Love...Earth's Most Delightful Prison...That You Never Want To Leave.©
#drMM

TW425 #"TWITTER"_TALK:
When I See Who Others Enjoy...I Don't Feel
Quite So Special...©
#drMM

TW426 #MAN_TALK:
#Thoughts For The Uncommon Men At The
Wisdom Center
1. Keep "The Little Boy" In You Alive
2. Investments~#1 Mind, #2 Wife©
#drMM

TW427 If You Follow My Instructions...You
Will Never Be #*Wrong.*
If You Don't Follow My Instructions...You
Will Never Be *Right.*©
#drMM

TW428 #TEAM_TALK:
Good People...Are Not Always Good *Workers.*
Good Workers...Are Not Always Good *People.*©
#drMM

TW429 AT 64-WHAT I DON'T WANT
AROUND ME:
~The *Non-Listener*-Saying "I Love You!"

~#*Uncaring*-On Payroll
~#*Unteachable*-Asking For Job©
#drMM

TW430 #"TWITTER"_TALK:
I Follow....For A #*Season*
I Unfollow...For A #*Reason*
I #Block...When I Smell *Treason*©
#drMM

TW431 YOU DON'T BELONG...
...Where Your #Words Are Not Heard.
...Where Your #Opinion Is Ignored.
...Where Your #Comfort Does Not Matter.©
#drMM

TW432 THE MYSTERY of #LIFE...Is
Knowing When To Impart Or...*Depart.*©
(ie. #Jesus~"Freely #Give" vs "Shake Dust")
#drMM

TW433 #PROTÉGÉ_TALK:
Acknowledgement...*Is Not Honor.*©
(Even *Flies* Are Acknowledged...)
#drMM

TW434 #RELATIONSHIPS:
The *Higher* The Quality...The *Fewer* You
Need.©
#drMM

TW435 In Discovering Those Who Dislike
Me; I Discover That I Have The SAME
Feelings...Toward Them!
Agreement!
Ahhh...Such #Peace.©
#drMM

TW436 CARING IS...
...An #Anointing, Not A Feeling
...Instantly Discernable
...Magnifies The Uncaring
...*Irreplaceable*©
#drMM

TW437 FATHER, Remind Us To #Think...
WORLD-CLASS...
As We Represent You *Graciously*
~In Our *#Reactions*
~In Every *#Conversation.*©
#drMM

TW438 #ACCESS...Is The Greatest Gift Possible On Earth.
...An #*Invitation* To Relationship
...An #*Opportunity* To Reveal Love©
#drMM

TW439 #ACCESS...Is Oxygen For Love
...The Stage Where *Passion* Performs
...Where #*Reactions* Expose
...Where #*Words* / *Tone* Reveal #Focus.©
#drMM

TW440 #ACCESS:
...Makes Caring *Measureable*
...Makes #Loyalty *Undoubtable*
...*Reveals* Hidden Needs.©
#drMM

TW441 #PROTÉGÉ_TALK:
Place Great Importance On ACCESS
~The Master Gift
~#Moment of Opportunity
~Portrait of You
~Proof of #Favor©
#drMM

TW442 #LEADERSHIP_TALK:
#ACCESS...Checklist Test For Assessment
~#Relationship Potential
~#Team Compatibility
~#Wisdom In Reactions©
#drMM

TW443 #ACCESS...Reveals In A *Moment*
More Than A Thousand Commendations
Can Reveal In A *Lifetime.*©
#drMM

TW444 A #Moment of ACCESS...Can
Remove The Confusion of 1,000 #Love
Letters.©
#drMM

TW445 #PROTÉGÉ_TALK:
#ACCESS Is *#Opportunity.*©
~Joseph...Had One #Conversation To
  Impress Pharoah
~Esther...Had Two Meals To *#Change* A
  King©
#drMM

TW446 7 EXPLANATIONS For YOUR
#LIFE SITUATION:
...Economy
...Fate
...#Luck
...Destiny
...God Predestined
...Your #Parents
...Your #Decisions©
#drMM

TW447 #IMAGINE:
...Discovering The REAL Reason God
  Created You & Where You Belong.
...Meeting Someone #Craving...Your
  #Difference.©
#drMM

TW448 #RELATIONSHIP-KILLER:
~When You *Demand* From Someone...
Something They Do Not Possess.©
(#Time-#$$-#Love-#Romance-Servitude)
#drMM

TW449 REASONS PEOPLE ARE
IGNORED:

~Tone of *#Disrespect*
~#Desire For Useless *Argument*
~A *Distorted Perception* of #Relationship©
#drMM

TW450 #FORGIVENESS:
...Does Not Guarantee They Will Change
...Does Not Make Them Trustworthy
...Permits #God To Penalize.©
#drMM

TW451 WORLD CUP:
That Glorious #Time When A Husband Can
Watch His #Wife Squeal With Excitement
Over *Other* #Men.©
#drMM

TW452 6 THINGS #MEN WANT IN A
#WOMAN:
1~WOW Factor..!
2~#Trustworthiness
3~#Fear of God
4~#Entertainment
5~#Admiration
6~#Kindness©
#drMM

TW453 3 THINGS #MEN HATE IN A #WOMAN
1. #Correction
2. Correction
3. *Correction*©
#drMM

TW454 #PROTOCOL:
Don't Take Anything...That Is Not Given To You.©
(#Authority-Position-Role In #Relationship)
#drMM

TW455 PRAYER FOR PASTORS:
Father, As We Sow Our #Persuasions
Enable Us To #FOCUS On
The *Crushed*...Not Critics
#Reachers, Not Rebels.©
#drMM

TW456 #PROTÉGÉ_TALK:
Whose #Counsel Matters To You?
What Present #Weakness Could Destroy You?
Who Has Invested The Most In You?©
#drMM

TW457 #FATHER,
Help Me Be *Right,* Not Just Different.
Teach Me *Graciousness,* Not Just #Integrity.
Make Me A *Healer,* Not Just A #Teacher.©
#drMM

TW458 TO #ATHEIST:
I Ache For You...Because, I Too, Have Lived
In #Doubt...Unspeakable #Disappointment
In People-
#Change...*Happens.*©
#drMM

TW459 #Gentleness...Is Never Inappropriate.
Ever.©
#drMM

TW460 MR. #ATHEIST...
...The Customers At Your Store Don't Seem
To Be Too #Happy...Like The Ones In *The
#Jesus Line.*©
#drMM

TW461 MR. #ATHEIST...
Your Unhappiness Does Not *Excite* Me.©
#drMM

TW462 #PROTÉGÉ_TALK:
Energy & #Time Are Two #Investments You
Must *Never* Make...
...In *#Fools* Nor *Adversaries.*©
#drMM

TW463 Be Neither #Angry Nor #Bitter
With Behavior of #Fools.
Be Thankful.
Very.
But For #Grace of God~That Could Be *You.*©
#drMM

TW464 3 DANGER SIGNALS-USA:
~#Disrespect For Israel
~#Contempt For Christianity
~#Cowardice Toward Confrontation©
#drMM

TW465 I WONDER...
~What Hidden #Prejudice Lies Dormant
  Within Me...*Undetected?*
~What Small #Decision...Could Create A
  Huge #Change?©
#drMM

TW466 CONSCIENCE:
Who Has Invested The *Most* IntoYou?
(Energy~#Time~$$~Patience)
What Has Been Their *#Reward?*
Does It *Matter* To YOU?©
#drMM

TW467 FOCUS:
An *Effective* YES...Will Always Require *100*
No's.©
#drMM

TW468 SOMEDAY...You Will #Believe...
Someone..!
That Day Will Decide...What You Become
For The Rest of Your #Life.
Who...Have You #Decided To Believe?©
#drMM

TW469 #FINANCES:
#Money Is Not A Miracle.
Money Is Not A Mystery.
Money Is...Simply The *#Reward System* For
Solving #Problems.©
#drMM

TW470 #SUCCESS:
Picture...Lifestyle You *Desire*.
Pursue...#Mentorship From Who You *Admire*.
#Plan...Changes In Daily #Success *Routine*.©
#drMM

TW471 #FUTURE:
Are You *Racing* Toward Your #Future To
Experience A Feeling...
...That Is *Already* Available In Your
PRESENT?©
#drMM

TW472 #PROTÉGÉ_TALK:
Master...#Art_of_RECEIVING.
Identify #Gifts...From God/Parents/All.
Exude #Gratitude...For Deposits Into You.©
#drMM

TW473 #RECEIVING:
1) #ACCESS...As Gift & Test
2) #INSTRUCTION...As An Opportunity To
Prove Your Passion/Competence/
Understanding©
#drMM

`TW474` #PASTORAL_TALK:
3 Good Decisions...
~*Train* Team Via Personal DVD's
~*Replace* Disloyalty Swiftly/Quietly
~*Identify* Your "Elisha"©
#drMM

`TW475` 3 SECRETS TO #FAVOR WITH YOUR BOSS:
1. Follow His Instructions
2. Follow His Instructions
3. *Follow His Instructions*©
#drMM

`TW476` #SINGLE_TALK:
When I Know What You *Enjoy*...I Can Predict Our *Future.*
When I Know Who You *Honor*...I Can Predict My *Joy.*©
#drMM

`TW477` 6 REACTIONS REVEAL #CHARACTER:
Your Reaction To...
~#Correction
~#Instructions

~#Authority
~#Mistakes
~#Gifts
~#Bible©
#drMM

TW478 3 DECISIONS THAT CREATE
#SUCCESS:
~Who You Decide To *Honor*
~Weakness You Decide To *Overcome*
~Voice You Decide To *Trust*©
#drMM

TW479 #SINGLE_TALK:
The Right One Will Not...
ENDURE Your #Difference.
The Right One Will...
REQUIRE Your Difference.©
#drMM

TW480 #DearSis:
Has He Discussed His Most Serious
Weakness?
Are You At Peace With His History?
Do You Know His True Financial State?©
#drMM

TW481 #DearSis:
Is YOUR Opinion...Pursued?
Do You #Love...What Excites Him?
Have You Ever Heard Him #Lie To Anyone?©
#drMM

TW482 #DearSis:
What #Questions Does He Not Answer?
What Is His #Relationship With Pastor?
Do You Know His #Financial History?©
#drMM

TW483 #ASSIGNMENT:
Everything Created...*Solves* A #Problem.
Your Assignment...Is *Geographical*.
You Are A #Reward...To *Someone*.©
#drMM

TW484 #SINGLE_TALK:
All #Men Do Not Want The Same Thing In
A #Woman.
Some Men Merely Want An Experience...*Not*
A #*Relationship*.©
#drMM

TW485 WHAT I #LISTEN FOR...IN A
#WOMAN:
~Whose #Comfort Matters (Rebekkah)
~Quality of Her #Questions (Queen of Sheba)
~Who #Trained Her (Ruth)©
#drMM

TW486 #QUESTIONS:
Who Succeeded This Year...Because of YOU?
What Will Be Your Legacy...In ONE Word?
What Is #Success...*To You?*©
#drMM

TW487 #SUCCESS:
1~The Proof of Success Is...#*Joy.*
2~Success...Is A *Daily* Experience.
3~Your Success Is Not...A Divine
#Decision.©
#drMM

TW488 #GOVERNMENT:
#Evil Is Not An Act.
Evil Is A *Philosophy.*
Observe...The *Changing* of #Laws.©
#drMM

TW489 #SEASONS... Are Decided By #Conversations.©
#drMM

TW490 #IDEAS:
1~Create A *Tomorrow* Room. (Pictures of #Future #Goals)
2~Choose *One* Topic To Master.
3~Keep List of *#Questions.*©
#drMM

TW491 #WORSHIP_LEADERS:
When You Stir People To SING...
~Their CHAINS Are *Broken.*
~Their #FOCUS Is *Corrected.*
~Their #HOPE *Returns.*©
#drMM

TW492 #PROBLEMS:
...Are *Invitations* To #Relationship.
...Are *Seeds* For #Favor.
...*Decide* Your Salary.
...*Reveal* Your #Difference.©
#drMM

TW493 #DISTRUST...Is Often A Divine *Signal* For Your *Safety.*©
#drMM

TW494 #RELATIONSHIPS:
Sometimes...Just A Sip *Satisfies.*©
#drMM

TW495 HELL:
I Fear Not The Fire; But Being With Every #Fool In The Universe At The Same #Time Is...*Absolute Torment.*©
#drMM

TW496 #INEXPERIENCE...Cannot Be Hidden.
Inexperience+#Humility=*Possibility*©
#drMM

TW497 DON'T #BLOCK...The #Atheist;
He May #Follow You All The Way To #Heaven.©
#drMM

TW498 ECSTACY...To A #Giver Is
Discovering Someone *Qualified* To Receive.©
#drMM

TW499 YOUR NEXT #SEASON...Is Only
One Person Away.©
Rebekah/Eleazar/Isaac
Joseph/Butler/Pharoah
Ruth/Naomi/Boaz
#drMM

TW500 QUESTIONS:
~When You Get Where You Are Going...
  Where Will You Be?
~When You Get What You Want...*What* Will
  You Have?©
#drMM

TW501 JOBLESS?
Interviewing #Bosses Love To Hear:
You Will Never Have To Repeat
#Instructions To Me.
I Am A *Completer..!*©
#drMM

TW502 #MATE:
No Well #Woman Will Stay...With An Abuser.
No Well #Man Will Stay...With An Abuser.
Anything Permitted...*Increases.*©
#drMM

TW503 #LOVE...Is #Seed For #Happiness.
Doing~The Work/Job You Love.
Talking~About #Passion You Love.
Giving~To Someone You Love.©
#drMM

TW504 #SINGLE_TALK:
#Love_Signs...
~Their Reactions Decide For You.
~Their Simplest Texting Excites You.
~You Dread Their Leaving.©
#drMM

TW505 #IMAGINE:
...The Children You Could Feed If You
Really, Really Prospered.
...The Possibility of #Money...If YOU Had It.©
#drMM

TW506 #SINGLE_TALK:
Some...Allow Their Loneliness To Choose
Their #Mate.
The #Wise...Allow Their #JOY To Choose
Their Mate.©
#drMM

TW507 Are You *#Ignorant*...Or #Stupid?
Ignorant...Not Knowing.
Stupid...Not ASKING.©
#drMM

TW508 #SUBMISSION...Is Not Ownership.
Submission...Is *Permission* To Protect.©
#drMM

TW509 #IMAGINE:
...What You Would Find If You Focused ALL
of You On ONLY One Thing.
...What You Have NEVER Experienced.
Imagine.©
#drMM

TW510 About #ATHEISTS...It's Hard For
Me To Criticize Those...Who Have Not Had
My Experiences.
Even God-Experiences.©
#drMM

TW511 #THINK...
SOMETHING Already In Your Present...
May Give You The #Pleasure You Think...Is
Hidden In Your #Future.© #drMM

TW512 SELF-CARE:
The Happiest You...Is The *Greatest* #Gift
You Can Give *Others.*©
(So...Invest Heavily In Your Own Joy)
#drMM

TW513 #Friendship Is Too Valuable...To
Offer To The Scornful.©
(So Use #Unfollow & #Block *Without*
Hesitation)
#drMM

TW514 MY 5 UNBEARABLES:
1. #Deception
2. #Disrespect
3. #Ingratitude
4. #Uncaring
5. #Non_Listeners©
(Find Your 5 Too~Saves #Time)
#drMM

TW515 #PASSION:
Whatever Is Not Your #QUEST...Will Never
Become Your Experience.©
(Ask/Seek/Knock...Need Is Not A Qualifier)
#drMM

TW516 $$
I Am Astounded That Those So Critical
Toward #Prosperity...Have Still Not
Discovered The Divine Reason For It.©
#drMM

TW517 #CONVERSATION:
Your #*Words*...Affect My #*Mind*.
Your *Tone*...Affects My #*Heart*.©
#drMM

TW518 #PROTÉGÉ_TALK:
#Honor Creates Access...Into ANY
#Environment
Honor Creates...What Genius Cannot.
#Learn THIS~It's Enough.©
#drMM

TW519 #DearSis:
Don't *Pursue* A #Man You Don't #*Trust*.
Don't *Correct* A Man Who Didn't *Ask*.
Don't #*Mentor* A Man You Won't #*Follow*.©
#drMM

TW520 #BITTERNESS...Is The #Seed For
Loss. (Access/Job/Friendship)

#Bitterness Is Deadlier Than Betrayal.
(Internal/External)©
#drMM

TW521 #CONVERSATION:
#*Talk* To Me~I Will *Listen.*
Talk To Me *Kindly*~I Will *Respond.*
Talk To Me With #*Honor*~I May *Become*
Your #Friend.©
#drMM

TW522 YOU...
#God Made You What You WERE.
You Became...What You *Are.*
Now, You Can Become...Whatever You
#*Admire.*©
#drMM

TW523 3 ZONES of #TRUST:
1. #Caring...(Mother)
2. #Competence...(Surgeon)
3. #Character...(Mate)©
#drMM

TW524 #CONVERSATION:
Reveals...

~If My Comfort Matters.
~How Long I'd Enjoy You.
~What You Consider Important.
~Perception of Me.©
#drMM

`TW525` #PROTÉGÉ_TALK:
Invest VERY Carefully...
~Your #Energy
~#Conversations
~#Money
~#Time
~#Counsel©
(I Regret 50% of My Investments)
#drMM

`TW526` YOU:
You Don't #Decide What You Need...You
#DISCOVER What You Need.©
#drMM

`TW527` #SINGLE_TALK:
When You Explained What You Needed...I
Realized I Wasn't.©
#drMM

TW528 #RELATIONSHIPS:
Those Who HEAR You...Should Be The Only
Ones NEAR You.©
#drMM

TW529 #SINGLE_TALK:
If You #Listen Well...*One* #Conversation
Will Often Reveal *Enough*.©
#drMM

TW530 #CONVERSATION:
What People Say Doesn't Agitate Me; Their
Saying To ME...Agitates Me.©
#drMM

TW531 #CONVERSATION:
The #Father Never Intended For You To
#Succeed...Without CONTINUOUS
Conversations With Him.© (Deut 4:34)
#drMM

TW532 #"TWITTER"_TALK:
Sometimes I FOLLOW Someone Interesting...
Only To Discover They Are Going Somewhere
That I Am *Not*.©
#drMM

TW533 #DESTINY:
#Hell Is Proof That Destiny...*Is Purely Optional.*©
#drMM

TW534 #MENTORSHIP:
Exhaustion: Thrusting A *Cup* of #Knowledge...Into A *Spoon* Mind.©
#drMM

TW535 #QUESTION:
#God Is In Control..!!!!
of What..?©
#drMM

TW536 #DECEPTION:
At 24...I *Confronted* #Liars.
At 64...I Simply *Identify* Them.©
(Never Tell Thieves Where Security Cameras Are.)
#drMM

TW537 WHO #God Controls Differs From...WHAT He Controls.
He Has Never Made A Human #Decision.©
#drMM

TW538 #DESTINY:
If Everything Is Predestined...
...#Obedience Creates No Change.
...#Wisdom Is Unnecessary.
...#Prayer Is Useless.©
#drMM

TW539 #MOMENTS:
Don't *Rush* Away From The Present
#Moment...It Took You A *Lifetime* To Get
Here.©
#drMM

TW540 #LOVE IS...Whatever You Cannot
Walk Away From.©
#drMM

TW541 #SINGLE_TALK:
#Love Is...KIND.©
(Further Commentary/#Conversation/
Exploration Is Unnecessary)
#drMM

TW542 #IMAGINE:
...If You Mastered The Art_of_#Receiving...

Like You Mastered #Giving.
...If Every #Seed You Sowed Was In Good
Soil.©
#drMM

TW543 #LOVE IS...A *Divine*
#Assignment.©
#drMM

TW544 #LOVE IS...Discovering *Where* To
Invest Your #LIFE.©
#drMM

TW545 #LAW_of_RECOGNITION
You Are Like A Christmas Tree...And Most
Presents #God Has Sent You Remain
Unopened.©
#drMM

TW546 #QUESTIONS:
Have You Counted The Cost of *Unanswered*
#Questions?
~Who Could You Have *Loved?*
~Who Should You Have *Trusted?*©
#drMM

TW547 #SINGLE_TALK:
#Heart_Talk Here...#Love Is Too Glorious
To Leave...*Unmastered.*
Singleness...May Be *Unnatural.*©
(ie. Unrest)
#drMM

TW548 #RELATIONSHIPS:
If I Keep Avoiding Negative People...
Who Will #Mentor Them..?©
#drMM

TW549 WHY...Are You Not Pursuing What
You *Really* Want..?©
#drMM

TW550 I Am Trying Hard...To Understand
The #Passion & #Goal of Those Who *Hate*
#Prosperity-Teaching.©
(Is Poverty That *Fulfilling?*)
#drMM

TW551 WHAT PART OF THE #BIBLE...
Have You Decided Not To #Believe?
(It May Be Linked To What Is *Missing* In
Your Life.)© #drMM

TW552 #SINGLE_TALK:
#Caring...Is Not An Instruction To #*Marry*
Someone.
Caring...Is Often An #Instruction To
Intercede.©
#drMM

TW553 I Am Trying Hard...To Understand
Why The Anti-Prosperity Christian Doesn't
Have *Same* #Anger Toward Poverty~Drugs~
Liquor.©
#drMM

TW554 THE CLOSEST THING TO
SATAN...Is Often A *Misguided* Christian.©
#drMM

TW555 #SISTER_TALK:
Know His *Heart*...Before You Get Into His
Face.©
#drMM

TW556 #PROTOCOL:
Never Enter...*Uninvited.*©
#drMM

TW557 #LOVE IS...Discovering *Where* To Invest Your #LIFE.©
#drMM

TW558 #PROSPERITY:
...Is The Tool of Dreamers
...Is A Weapon For #Warriors
...Is The #Reward For Honoring Divine Laws©
(Deut 28)
#drMM

TW559 #GOD...
Which Part of God...Have *You* Experienced?
Which Part of God...Have You NOT Experienced?
Never *Argue* The Unknown.©
#drMM

TW560 #PROSPERITY:
...Is Having Enough Provision
~ To #Obey A Divine Instruction
~ To Complete Your #Assignment©
#drMM

Miracle 7 BOOK PAK!

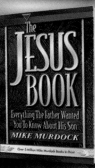

❶ Dream Seeds (Book/B-11/106pg/$12)

❷ 7 Hidden Keys to Favor (Book/B-119/32pg/$7)

❸ Seeds of Wisdom on Miracles (Book/B-15/32pg/$3)

❹ Seeds of Wisdom on Prayer (Book/B-23/32pg/$3)

❺ The Jesus Book (Book/B-27/166pg/$10)

❻ The Memory Bible on Miracles (Book/B-208/32pg/$3)

❼ The Mentor's Manna on Attitude (Book/B-58/32pg/$3)

DR. MIKE MURDOCK

The Wisdom Center
Miracle 7 Book Pak!
Only $**30** $41 Value
WBL-24
Wisdom Is The Principal Thing

Add 20% For S/H

Quantity Prices Available Upon Request

Each Wisdom Book may be purchased separately if so desired.

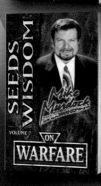

Money 7 BOOK PAK!

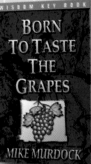

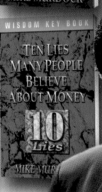

DR. MIKE MURDOCK

1. **Secrets of the Richest Man Who Ever Lived** (Book/B-99/179pg/$15)

2. **The Blessing Bible** (Book/B-28/252pg/$10)

3. **Born To Taste The Grapes** (Book/B-65/32pg/$3)

4. **Creating Tomorrow Through Seed-Faith** (Book/B-06/32pg/$5)

5. **Seeds of Wisdom on Prosperity** (Book/B-22/32pg/$5)

6. **Seven Obstacles To Abundant Success** (Book/B-64/32pg/$5)

7. **Ten Lies Many People Believe About Money** (Book/B-04/32pg/$5)

*Each Wisdom Book may be purchased separately if so desired.

The Wisdom Center
Money 7 Book Pak!
Only $30
$48 Value
WBL-30
Wisdom Is The Principal Thing

Add 20% For S/H

THE WISDOM CENTER
4051 Denton Highway • Fort Worth, TX 76117

1-817-759-BOOK
1-817-759-2665
1-817-759-0300

You Will Love Our Website..!
WISDOMONLINE.COM   C

Career 7

Book Pak For Business People!

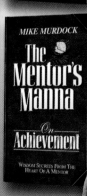

DR. MIKE MURDOCK

1. **The Businessman's Topical Bible** (Book/B-33/384pg/$10)

2. **31 Secrets for Career Success** (Book/B-44/112pg/$12)

3. **31 Scriptures Every Businessman Should Memorize** (Book/B-141/32pg/$3)

4. **7 Overlooked Keys To Effective Goal-Setting** (Book/B-127/32pg/$7)

5. **7 Rewards of Problem Solving** (Book/B-118/32pg/$8)

6. **How To Double Your Productivity In 24 Hours** (Book/B-137/32pg/$7)

7. **The Mentor's Manna on Achievement** (Book/B-79/32pg/$5)

*Each Wisdom Book may be purchased separately if so desired.

The Wisdom Center
Career 7 Book Pak!
Only $**30**
$52 Value
WBL-27
Wisdom Is The Principal Thing

Add 20% S&H

D

THE WISDOM CENTER
4051 Denton Highway • Fort Worth, TX 76117

1-817-759-BOOK
1-817-759-2665
1-817-759-0300

You Will Love Our Website..!
WISDOMONLINE.COM

Unforgettable Woman 4
Book Pak!

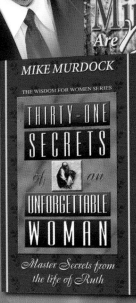

1 Where Miracles Are Born (Book/B-115/32pg/$7)

2 Secrets of The Journey, Vol. 6 (Book/B-102/32pg/$5)

3 Thirty-One Secrets of an Unforgettable Woman (Book/B-57/140pg/$12)

4 The Proverbs 31 Woman (Book/B-49/70pg/$7)

The Wisdom Center
Unforgettable Woman 4 Book Pak!
Only **$20** $31 Value
PAK-31
Wisdom Is The Principal Thing

Add 20% For S/H

ch Wisdom Book may be purchased separately if so desired.

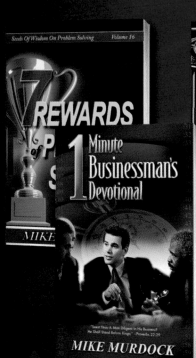

CHAMPIONS 4
Book Pak!

Secrets of the Journey

MY PERSONAL DREAM BOOK

Wisdom For Crisis Times
Master Keys For Success In Times Of Change
MIKE MURDOCK

The Making of A *CHAMPION*
31 Power Keys To Unleashing Your Personal Greatness
MIKE MURDOCK
A 31 DAY MENTORSHIP PROGRAM OF WISDOM

❶ **Secrets of The Journey, Vol. 3** (Book/B-94/32pg/$5)

❷ **My Personal Dream Book** (Book/B-143/32pg/$5)

❸ **Wisdom For Crisis Times**
(Book/B-40/112pg/$12)

❹ **The Making of A Champion**
(Book/B-59/128pg/$12)

The Wisdom Center
Champions 4 Book Pak!
Only $20 $34 Value
Wisdom Is The Principal Thing
PAK-23

Each Wisdom Book may be purchased separately if so desired.

Add 20% For S/H

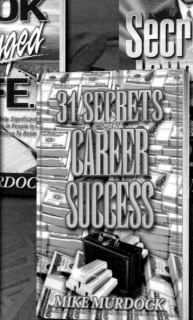

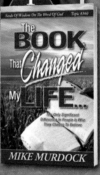

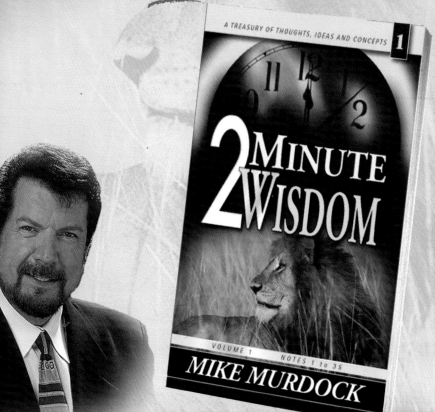

THE WISDOM BIBLE
Partnership Edition

Over 120 Wisdom Study Guides Included Such As:

- ▶ *10 Qualities of Uncommon Achievers*
- ▶ *18 Facts You Should Know About The Anointing*
- ▶ *21 Facts To Help You Identify Those Assigned To You*
- ▶ *31 Facts You Should Know About Your Assignment*
- ▶ *8 Keys That Unlock Victory In Every Attack*
- ▶ *22 Defense Techniques To Remember During Seasons of Personal Attack*
- ▶ *20 Wisdom Keys And Techniques To Remember During An Uncommon Battle*
- ▶ *11 Benefits You Can Expect From God*
- ▶ *31 Facts You Should Know About Favor*
- ▶ *The Covenant of 58 Blessings*
- ▶ *7 Keys To Receiving Your Miracle*
- ▶ *16 Facts You Should Remember About Contentious People*
- ▶ *5 Facts Solomon Taught About Contracts*
- ▶ *7 Facts You Should Know About Conflict*
- ▶ *6 Steps That Can Unlock Your Self-Confidence*
- ▶ *And Much More!*

Your Partnership makes such a difference in The Wisdom Center Outreach Ministries. I wanted to place a Gift in your hand that could last a lifetime for you and your family...**The Wisdom Study Bible.**

40 Years of Personal Notes...this Partnership Edition Bible contains 160 pages of my Personal Study Notes...that could forever change your Bible Study of The Word of God. This **Partnership Edition...**is my personal **Gift of Appreciation** when you sow your Sponsorship Seed of $1,000 to help us complete The Prayer Center and TV Studio Complex. An Uncommon Seed Always Creates An Uncommon Harvest!

Mike

Thank you from my heart for your Seed of Obedience (Luke 6:38).

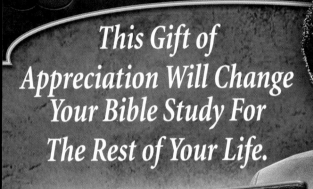

This Gift of Appreciation Will Change Your Bible Study For The Rest of Your Life.

The Wisdom Bible

MY GIFT OF APPRECIATION
Celebrating Your Sponsorship Seed of $1,000 For The Prayer Center & TV Studio Complex
B-235
Wisdom Is The Principal Thing

 THE WISDOM CENTER 4051 Denton Highway • Fort Worth, TX 76117

1-817-759-BOOK
1-817-759-2665
1-817-759-0300

You Will Love Our Website..!
WISDOMONLINE.COM

M

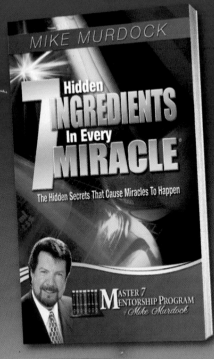

YOUR ASSIGNMENT IS YOUR DISTINCTION FROM OTHERS.

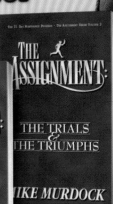

Assignment 4 Book Pak!

Uncommon Wisdom For Discovering Your Life Assignment.

❶ The Dream & The Destiny
Vol 1 (Book/B-74/164 pg/$15)

❷ The Anointing & The Adversity
Vol 2 (Book/B-75/192 pg/$12)

❸ The Trials & The Triumphs
Vol 3 (Book/B-97/160 pg/$12)

❹ The Pain & The Passion
Vol 4 (Book/B-98/144 pg/$12)

Each Wisdom Book may be purchased separately if so desired.

The Wisdom Center
Assignment 4 Book Pak!
Only $**30** $51 Value
WBL-14
Wisdom Is The Principal Thing

Add 20% For S/H

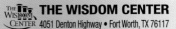
THE WISDOM CENTER
4051 Denton Highway • Fort Worth, TX 76117

1-817-759-BOOK
1-817-759-2665
1-817-759-0300

You Will Love Our Website..!
WISDOMONLINE.COM

O

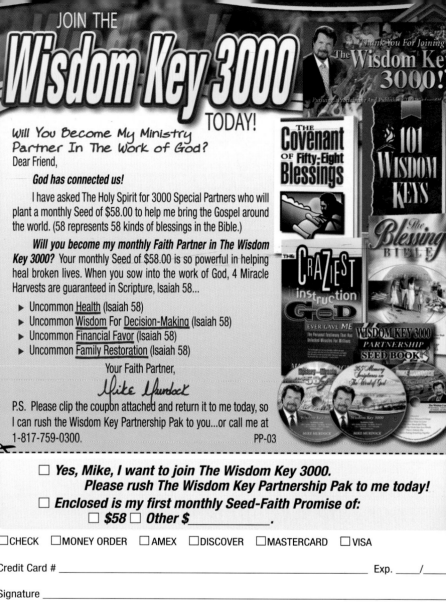

JOIN THE
Wisdom Key 3000
TODAY!

Thank You For Joining
The Wisdom Key 3000!
Pursuing, Proclaiming And Publishing The Wisdom Of God

Will You Become My Ministry Partner In The Work of God?
Dear Friend,

God has connected us!

I have asked The Holy Spirit for 3000 Special Partners who will plant a monthly Seed of $58.00 to help me bring the Gospel around the world. (58 represents 58 kinds of blessings in the Bible.)

Will you become my monthly Faith Partner in The Wisdom Key 3000? Your monthly Seed of $58.00 is so powerful in helping heal broken lives. When you sow into the work of God, 4 Miracle Harvests are guaranteed in Scripture, Isaiah 58...

- ▶ Uncommon <u>Health</u> (Isaiah 58)
- ▶ Uncommon <u>Wisdom</u> For <u>Decision-Making</u> (Isaiah 58)
- ▶ Uncommon <u>Financial Favor</u> (Isaiah 58)
- ▶ Uncommon <u>Family Restoration</u> (Isaiah 58)

Your Faith Partner,

Mike Murdock

P.S. Please clip the coupon attached and return it to me today, so I can rush the Wisdom Key Partnership Pak to you...or call me at 1-817-759-0300.   PP-03

☐ **Yes, Mike, I want to join The Wisdom Key 3000.**
   Please rush The Wisdom Key Partnership Pak to me today!
☐ **Enclosed is my first monthly Seed-Faith Promise of:**
      ☐ **$58** ☐ **Other $_____.**

☐ CHECK   ☐ MONEY ORDER   ☐ AMEX   ☐ DISCOVER   ☐ MASTERCARD   ☐ VISA

Credit Card # _____ Exp. ____/____

Signature _____

Name _____ Birth Date ____/____

Address _____

City _____ State _____ Zip _____

Phone _____ Email _____

Your Seed-Faith Offerings are used to support The Wisdom Center, and all of its programs. The Wisdom Center reserves the right to redirect funds as needed in order to carry out our charitable purpose. In the event The Wisdom Center receives more funds for the project than needed, the excess will be used for another worthy outreach. (Your transactions may be electronically deposited.)

P **THE WISDOM CENTER**
The WISDOM CENTER 4051 Denton Highway • Fort Worth, TX 76117

1-817-759-BOOK
1-817-759-2665
1-817-759-0300

— You Will Love Our Website..!
WISDOMONLINE.COM